Mentally Caged: Mental Health Stories from Prison
Copyright © 2022-2023 by Bruce LeMaster
Cover Art by Tess Pruim

Table of Contents:

Foreword:

When perusing the comment sections on pages and groups dedicated to any and all things True Crime, what stands out is the ubiquitously hostile disposition towards the offenders whose lives and crimes we all so vigorously discuss.

Even many of those who take an anti-death penalty stance appear to be of the opinion that inmates ought to suffer, both mentally and physically, believing that the primary function of a prison sentence should be to punish the convict.

There appear to be three main reasons for people to come to this conclusion. One is retribution, and amongst the people calling for it are yet two more predominant subsections in terms of reasoning:

Those who were victimized themselves at some point and who speak out of hurt, fear or anger. Furthermore, there are those who project their own pervasive aggression onto inmates, whom I have, in the past, dubbed "anger excitation consumers" of True Crime. In case of the latter, they may subconsciously consider themselves righteous because they managed to redirect their own aggression towards those who acted out their violent urges or fantasies. In other cases, there may be a hefty level of suppressed guilt about their own anger management issues involved, creating a vicious cycle. For while the rage directed at the inmates serves to alleviate their own anger, it also serves to reinforce and remind them of the fact they can neither tame nor rid themselves of it indefinitely.

The second reason for people to call for the government to obstinately mete out eternal punishment to offenders is the argument of incapacitation. Once an offender is removed from the general population, there will be no more crime. Regrettably, this is a complete lapse of judgment because if we take organized crime as an example, not only will the member of a group, or gang, be immediately replaced, but there is typically enough crime occurring in prison. As well, as it pertains to incarcerated organized criminals, they are not seldom employed to carry out operations inside of the facility they're being held at for the group they already used to work at on the outside. For instance, they may work as drug dealers behind bars.

Last on the list is the rationale that punishment will deter a) people on the outside from engaging in crime and b) those who may still be paroled from committing future crimes. However, studies have shown that this is not so, and the recidivism rate for inmates in the US to re offend currently stands at approximately 50%.

For one, the majority of offenders, particularly serial killers or serial violent offenders, already came from an upbringing that they experienced as punishment. Childhood emotional, physical and sexual abuse or neglect are among the top commonalities that almost all of them share. Punishment is already all they know and expect of the world, reinforcing their impression that it takes brutality in order not to "go under" in the world and subsequently in prison.

Add to this that serial offenders are more prone to having suffered head trauma at some point in their lives, and even among those who did not, their brain structures often vastly differ from that of neurotypical ("normal") people. So what, then, works on the disordered if not punishment? From Hervey Cleckley to Robert D. Hare, Martha Stout and Michael H. Stone, we are being told by most established clinicians that disordered and/or violent people simply cannot change, that psychotherapy does not only not work on them but that they have a habit of playing mind and manipulation games with their therapists. Therapy, or any rehabilitation attempt, is wasted on those with little to no empathy. Talk about a metaphorical death sentence.

If that were true, though, Norway wouldn't have one of the lowest recidivism rates in the world at about 20% within a five year span. What does Norway do differently than the US? For one, inmates are considered and treated as human beings, not as numbers or creatures, as is more often customary in the US. They may cook and dine together with the correctional officers or watch television with them. There are also more prisons offering art and music therapy, group and individual therapy, as well as high school and college courses. Both therapy and education appear to play a large role in changing the lives and outlook of offenders – even of those with long-term prison sentences – for the better. To gain understanding of their own compulsions and crimes facilitates a more benign disposition towards themselves, which in turn influences how they treat others.

Consequentially, others treat them differently as well, creating a reward cycle that was shown to work particularly well on cluster B personalities behind bars. They may never experience affective empathy but may learn and apply cognitive empathy when dealing with others as well as situations that would previously have resulted in them acting out in some form or another.

Additionally, many offenders experience a sense of genuine control over their own lives once given the opportunity to educate themselves behind bars. They take pride in their achievements and learned skills, which add purpose and meaning to their lives. Thankfully, there are already initiatives such as the Bard Prison Initiative (BPI) that was started in New York State in 1999, which offer inmates the chance to take college classes. Their recidivism rate remains at 2% for those who graduated, and at 5% for those who did not graduate.

While I am certainly not advocating for the release of serial killers from prison, it still is my innermost conviction that hardly any of them are lost causes and undeserving of exactly that which they often may not themselves possess: Empathy. An approach that focuses on therapy and education would not cost more than what the US – and other countries with a punishment-based approach – are currently shelling out. Large sums of money are required for repairs because inmates habitually revolt, and for the treatment of injuries sustained by other inmates as well as correctional officers in some cases. A restructuring of the prison system would, based on my reading about modern European countries' successes, lower the crime rate within prisons and also serve to keep correctional officers safer from harm. Moreover, it would result in less drug use, hence dealing, as well as the mental and emotional need to self-medicate as a means of escaping from the bleakness and hopelessness of prison life was removed from the equation.

Reading the stories of the inmates who

shared with Bruce what it is like to be "mentally caged," to be belittled, tormented, humiliated, ignored, and either incorrectly or over-medicated, was a mentally strenuous task for me. The further I read, the more I wondered whether all those who demand and celebrate the suffering of the incarcerated are actually truly aware of the often horrendous conditions they live – or vegetate – in. Are they really incapable of realizing their own hypocrisy in demanding empathy for the victims, but denying the offenders – the previous victims of traumatic childhoods and/or brain injury and neurodiversities – the same? To empathize with the offenders does not negate having the utmost empathy with the victims and survivors of crime, as well as with their families, who just as dauntingly suffer. In my view, there is only one way to combat violence and aggression in general, and that is not to create more or call for more of the same.

Thus it is my utmost hope that this unique and requisite publication will attract a plethora of readers who may reevaluate their positions on this complex issue, and create a more genuine dialog based on reason and empathy between True Crime aficionados worldwide.

-Erin Banks, October 23, 2022.

Introduction:

Where do I start? I decided to do this project in the middle of 2022 after interviewing various prisoners for my podcast *Killer's Crawlspace*. One prisoner had told me there were roughly half of the population locked up with him that shouldn't be in prison but in a hospital getting the proper helped they needed. It left me speechless at first and made me think of how true his statement actually was.

There are probably many people reading this book and thinking most of these individuals are making the stuff up so people will feel sorry for them...that's not the case I feel. I personally suffer from bi-polar (type 2) and I understand the stigma that surrounds mental health because as a man I was told to suck it up and get over it. A lot of us deal with comments like that in the free world so why would it be any different when you're locked up?

Could you imagine how great the world would be if everyone got the proper help they needed? I feel a lot of crimes wouldn't happen if the person suffering actually was talked with and someone was there to get them help. We all deserve to get help when we need it. We shouldn't be made to feel ashamed for reaching out. We're all human and we all make mistakes, which some of them are worse than others...we're still human. Those terms look simple but still have a deeper meaning because we're all not perfect and we're subject to make a mistake at some point.

The rest of this project you will read words from people who are serving time, have served time, or worked in the prison field and seen things first hand. I want to thank each of them for allowing me to share their voice, their story and their suffering.

"The concept of "mental health" in our society is defined largely by the extent to which an individual behaves in accord with the needs of the system and does so without showing signs of stress."

-Ted "Unabomber" Kaczynski

Story 1:

Mental Health in prison-they tranquilize us. To good effect. Heavy meds to keep us calm, regardless of our individual diagnoses. There is MUCH mental illness in here. I have some of my own. I killed a man after not medicating mine correctly, and I see strains far worse than mine everywhere in here.

We have three psychologists in house for 700 inmates. We have one psychiatrist who we see on a television screen once every so often and who does the pill prescribing. Such is our treatment plan.

I understand why they would prioritize giving us meds that stifle aggressiveness over giving us actual therapy and making us "fit for society someday"-because they don't care about making us fit for society someday. Iowa is the land of lifers. Once you get the life sentence you are a cash cow for the state. Paying for meds to make us chill out is cheaper than getting us help.

It would make me laugh if the feds made the state spend their own money to rehabilitate us, regardless of our sentences. It would also very likely help me. I continue to battle my own mental health issues while simultaneously figuring out my particular mental disorder.

THAT SAID...I am grateful to be in a country where, after being convicted of murder, am housed, clothed and fed instead of just executed. Being given head meds that bring me peace from time to time are part of that package as well. Thank you for that. And that's not sarcasm. The life sentences Iowa give are ridiculous, inhuman and purely profit-based, but I can't complain about the conditions of my confinement. I may not get actual therapy for my mental illness, but I will survive.

-Eric Miller

Story 2:

Hi, my name is William Dathan Holbert. Most folks everywhere call me Wild Bill. I'm forty-two years old and from North Carolina originally. I was Central America's foremost professional killer (hitman) and cartel associate from 2006 until my arrest in 2010. Serving forty-six years in Panama's most dangerous and notorious prison, I'm twelve years into that sentence... man! That's a mouthful ain't it?

So, my dear friend Bruce invited me to write a piece about what mental health care is like in a third world prison. As I mentioned, I'm twelve years into my homicide bit, and I've done time in four of Panama's prisons during that time. I've lived in every security level of prison (minimum to extreme) at one time or another. My knowledge is pretty complete in respect to what Panama's prison system has to offer.

The short answer is that, in my experience, mental health is simply not addressed in any way whatsoever by Panama's prison system. I'll give an example that I witnessed first hand to impress that point on you, the reader

In, or about 2015, a young man named Steven was brought to the David Public Prison in Panama's Chiriquí province. I was housed there awaiting trial during that time.

It seems Steven, who by all accounts wasn't mentally well and was a bit "slow" to boot, had murdered his long-time care giver. While his care giver/guardian slept, Steven bashed her brains out with a big rock that had been on the porch of their home.

Steven was difficult, but not terribly bad off when they brought him to the prison. He could dress and bathe himself, he could eat and wash his plate. But, he was prone to early morning outbursts. Because of this, no one (no prisoner) would accept him in a cell. Many tried, but poor Steven couldn't be okay during the night hours.

Steven was not violent at that point. He was childlike and pitiful. The prison's answer to this problem was to chain Steven by one leg to the door of the clinic. He was given about three feet of chain between his leg and the barred door of the clinic. Steven was left twenty four hours a day in this condition.

Steven lived chained to the door of the clinic for over a year. Oftentimes in the night, a fat, evil, horrible guard named Christian Nuñez would come by and beat Steven with a billy club. I witnessed this first hand as my cell faced the clinic (cell D1).

Steven would urinate and defecate in the hall where he was perpetually chained. He had no other way to relieve himself. Nuñez's disgusting, fat ass would come by and beat Steven for shitting or pissing in the hall. The other prisoners thought this was great sport, laughing and cheering Núñez on as he beat poor chained Steven, nightly. The restrained man would cry and whimper, which prompted Núñez to beat him harder, to the delight of all the inmates.

I remember asking God to allow me to build a death camp in Panama to exterminate the whole lot of these horrible goblins, prisoners and guards. The spectacle of a fat, middle-aged man abusing a poor wicked creature for the gratification of a vulgar mob made me desire genocide for the entire lot of them. I will never forget how much I hated them all. What a horrible bunch of vile filth they truly were, the lot of them.

After about a year, Steven developed a habit that caused him to be moved to a more remote part of the prison. This poor creature began chronically masturbating in front of everyone. The nurses in the clinic were horrified.

Now, it didn't bother the clinic staff to see poor Steven chained like a dog with black eyes and bruises, that was hunky-dory. But, when the depraved young man whipped out a small penis to pleasure himself again... and again... and again... That was too much for their chaste modesty.

The clinic staff complained and had Steven chained in the outdoors, over by the kitchen to a beam. He was changing, becoming an animal. Before, Steven spoke often to anyone who would listen. But, by this time he had stopped talking altogether.

Chained outside in the sun and rain, Steven became violent. The once placid, childlike young fellow now often attacked people. He once tried to bite my leg as I walked by.

A "fellow" prisoner asked me in Spanish, "Bill you gunna let 'em get away with that? Kick his ass!"

I confused him when I responded with, "I swear to Almighty God that if I see anyone else hit that poor freak, I'm gunna accumulate another homicide charge. Try me dipshit!"

Steven was sent to a "manicomio" (lunatic asylum) soon after that. I remember when they stuffed him kicking, screaming and crying into the prison van. He didn't want to leave the yard where he had been chained. It was hell, but it had become his home. He was afraid to leave.

He came to prison in Panama in need of a little assistance, only. After about fourteen months of the "treatment", Steven was lost completely. What was left of him wasn't even recognizable as human. (Sigh)

THIS IS A TRUE STORY.

I'm Wild Bill. Y'all come visit me on Facebook at STONE JUG ENTERTAINMENT. If you want to know more about me, buy my prison memoir LONG LIVE THE KING WILD BILL, available on Amazon. Write me at longlivethekingwildbill@gmail.com

God bless you all. Jesus Christ loves you and I love you too.

-Brother Wild Bill Holbert, inmate and Prison Chaplain, La Nueva Joya Prison, Hell on Earth, September, 2022

Story 3:

Well I don't know where to start, but as for mental health I can't think of anything that would put me in that category even though I've been in trouble most of my life. I've never experienced mental breakdowns or just went off and started killing a person or a bunch of people. I did set a bunch of fires at one time, I even set one and laid back down in the bed, but was pulled out by the fire department. I was about thirteen at the time and don't know what I was thinking, but it couldn't have been good.

There used to be a mental health here, but they were all moved because too many of them were committing suicide so they no longer have mental health or seg. here.

Being locked up in a cell twenty-two hours a day can do things to a person, but that individual has to keep his mind occupied with positive reading and there are many topics to read, try to keep happy thoughts, write people there are many people you can write that will help you and love you for who you are. They will uplift your spirits mentality and spiritually. All we have to do is talk, but we as an individual have to take that step.

-Deryl Madison

Story 4:

I was not a happy kid. I wet the bed every night for more than a decade. In childhood my parents divorced, I was depressed, I faced the unfair wrath of bullies in school with no defense because I was weak-bodied. In my teens when hormones were introduced I was constantly confounded by the world around me as an alien to our planet might feel. I did not belong because I believed there was no one else like me. I was not handling my domestically fractured family situation well, then I was molested in what was supposed to be the guaranteed safest place besides maybe a church...though church, as we know, is not a safe haven for many altar boys. I fell under the thrall of true crime exploring all avenues of information like books, movies, even serial killer "baseball" cards. I was a nonviolent skinny kid with no real friends that found the wrong guide in life. It ultimately, only at the age of 18, guided my way to prison, then death row for murder.

I was first held in the police lockup. Cells under the department. Holding cells. Holding me and others for their arraignment of charges following our arrest for some offense. I was put in a single cell, no roommate. Cops came by to see me. Not talk to me but stare and talk among themselves about the teenager who killed another teenage in their city last night. They wanted to see if I looked like a monster. I did not. They did not mock me or jeer. They did however treat me like a specimen you study. It felt wrong because it was.

I was transported to a county jail. There I avoided the "bull pen" or group cell and was temporarily housed in segregation or "the hole". I had never been arrested before. Being locked in was jarring. Then, being exposed to other criminals was intimidating. Nothing prepared me for this. They fed me. They provided a toilet, a sink, a window, a bed. But at night they took my clothes because upon intake a correctional officer or "CO" spotted blood on my sock while strip-searching me upon intake, They left me naked a good half hour and now I was ridiculed by the other inmates who could see me. It was embarrassing and seemingly endless, I still remember that shame 25 years later.

My time in "county" was short-lived. I had been charged with capital felony and so was considered a "high security" inmate who required more restrictions than a county afforded its population. So they placed me in a so-called level 4 prison an hour away from the Massachusetts border. There came my 3rd strip search in life. This time it was done en masse. I was made to undress and go through motions as instructed by a CO like opening my mouth, messing up my hair, lifting my arms up, my scrotum, showing the bottoms of my feet, squatting and coughing (to dislodge any contraband that might be "embedded" in me) all in the presence of maybe half a dozen other inmates. They were simultaneously stripped and forced through these motions to insure nothing came into the prison but my flesh and bones. I would spend the next 20 months in this facility.

They made me live alone for 30 days before putting me in the cell with a complete stranger. I would go on to have multiple cellmates over the next near year and a half. Some easy to live with, more not. I was evaluated by a mental health department figure.

She was kind unlike the COs who reminded me daily why I was here by voice and action (searching my cell for supposed contraband 4 times a week.) This lady listened to me when I told her I was not sleeping well. She saw that I belonged here for my crimes but was not prepared for this environment. I was miserable as can be and losing weight from little meals. I soon after met with a shrink, of sorts. He asked all about my childhood then questioned me about how I was adapting to prison.

I had a sad and lonely childhood and being in prison only magnified the wretch that had walked into this building. For the first time in my now 19th year on earth, having just "celebrated" a birthday in the same room as a Latin King who shot someone to death (this young gang member was my cellmate) I was prescribed antidepressants. There would be side effects but my moods improved a little. The drugs messed with my libido which had been revved up with hormones fresh from puberty and the drugs made me perpetually lethargic. Half the day I was not sleeping I felt like I wanted to be sleeping. They were quick to medicate but beyond that initial evaluation I was never counseled or seen by a social worker. I was a teenager who committed a senseless murder and no one talked to me about how it might be affecting me.

At this facility where people go before they are either convicted or released from their charges I saw many abuses. Regularly inmates who were clearly incompatible were put in the same cell together always ending in a fight. Sometimes it was over after one exchange of blows. Sometimes there was a need for medical attention. There were numerous desperate attempts to commit suicide by hanging. Guys would collar themselves then tie the sheet to the bunk bed ladder and lower themselves to an awkward squat that would close their throat. They'd do this right when the CO would do his quarter hour tour of the unit/cell block so to be "rescued" and now made to be seen by mental health staff who had been ignoring them. My written requests to mental health always went unanswered. I only saw the shrink every 6 months to see if my medication should be adjusted. They set up this time table of twice a year whereas I could have benefited from such attention twice a week. Though my moods were not as extreme anymore I was still sad, remorseful, mourning my own short life, and perpetually frightened of an unknown future.

A jury of 12 determined that future to be brief when they elected the death penalty as a fitting sentence. I was then moved to a level 5 correctional institution everybody calls The Dungeon. There I went to death row.

On death row I reverted to a single cell status. The state did not put me in the cell with anyone else to insure nobody kills me before they can. I would stay in isolation with zero inmate contact for the next 22 years. In that time I won my appeal but remained in The Dungeon during my retrial which resulted, again, in death. Here I remained till the state abolished the death penalty.

In my decades in a cell alone I struggled to endure life. I flirted with religion, creatively explored art, became invested in TV and reflected nonstop on what brought me here. Some days were bad, some days were easier but none of them were good. Here, through all my

20s and 30s, I saw a revolving door of shrinks each experimenting on my mental health with a different drug. As if a pill would resolve my issues. All they needed to do was listen to me talk. But they were not here to hear me vent. They offered no counseling, just drugs. Some of these chemicals changed my body making it heavier at times, some turned me into a zombie, all affected my libido. If I thought the gawking police were bad or the COs in that first prison with their uncensored ridicule then The Dungeon offered a new breed of prison guard. Here they treated us condemned as one might treat the man who assaulted their grandma. They were awful human beings, and we were the ones locked up. I would spend my last day in The Dungeon in spring of 2021 having arrived in fall of 1999. I was transported to a level 4 facility a stone's throw from that first prison I spent 1997 to 1999 in.

Now I was in population beginning to interact with many other criminals at the age of 42. It's like I was the new guy but I had been doing time for as long as some of these men had been living. Here, mental health was different.

As usual, I was reevaluated. And this new doctor tried out a different drug on me. As I pen these words I take 4 different medications a day. Here, there is counseling and programs to better yourself. I am even enrolled in college classes. But here mental health is not dealt fairly. For some reason I am given attention and care. Multiple others' request to be seen, heard, treated fall on deaf ears.

My first celly worshiped Budda but had a definite problems in the attic. He rubbed Vaseline on the wall then rubbed his topless torso against it to moisturize. I said I'd help if he can't reach his back but he said that was weird. In my short time between arrest and conviction/death sentence, 20 months, I had multiple cellies/cellmates. One we'll call Alex was all Christian out of the cell and generous with his snacks to other inmates, real charitable, but in the cell at night he'd openly masturbate and beg me to suck him off. We were both 19. I dealt with mental health when nightmares plagued me. As a child I was haunted by nightmares, they returned with a vengeance in prison. Mental Health's solution was to sedate

me which put me right back in the clutches of
my nightmares. There was no talking about why
the nightmares had begun again just pills and
pills and pills.

-Joseph "Todd" Rizzo

Story 5:

On June 29, 2013 I asked to see mental health because my sister was going through some stuff with her cancer. It was making me depressed so I asked the DOC officer if I can see mental health and the officer told me to talk to the Lt when he comes and does his rounds. So when the Lt showed up I told him my problem and he told the officer to call mental health and see if they would see me and mental health told them to send me down.

So when I got there this guy came out and told me to come to his office so I started telling him my problem and he started acting like I was boring him. So I asked him am I boring you and the mental health guy said he does not know who my case worker is so I told him they have to get their shit together so he asked me what he wants him to do. I told him to just hear me out and stop acting like I'm boring you. He than told me to get out of his office and I said if I do something to somebody I don't want you asking me questions because I'm here telling you what my problem is and you are telling me to get out of your office.

So I left his office and then the officer that was at the desk asks me was I done and I said yes I'm done with that asshole and the CO took it as I was talking to him and told me I can't go back to my block that I was going to seg which means solitary confinement. I was put there for 3 days all the while I was down there I asked to see mental health and they kept telling me they don't have enough staff so I can't see anybody. After the 3 days the captain of the block came to talk to me and told me before I leave solitary confinement I will see mental health but I did not see anybody I even wrote the head person of mental health and she did not call me at all.

I had my aunt call up here in order for someone to see me and when I did see somebody I had to tell them I was saving all the requests I had written to their boss and I was going over their bosses' head. Mind you through all that I lost my job, but once I said that about their boss they then put me on meds.

Here is another story about mental health. There was a guy in seg and he was in a 4point restraint and he had to shit and he kept telling the COs he had to go , but they just acted like he was not there. So he shit himself and they left him there for a couple of hours until they did not want to smell him anymore. They then took a five gallon bucket of water and threw it on him to wash him off and all they had to do is take him to the showers.

There was a guy in my block and he kept on saying there's something wrong with his stomach for about a year and the medical department kept saying to him it's nothing but gas so the guy kept on telling medical he's still having problems after a year...it's been about a year and half now so the medical department said they are going to bring him to the outside hospital. The guy knew he was not coming back so he told us goodbye and he was right when the hospital found out what he had, they had to keep him in the hospital and when the hospital cut him open he died on the table. He had stomach cancer the whole time.

Another time about two weeks ago a guy

fell on his face and was not moving and about a dozen COs rushed to my block and all they did was stand around until medical showed up. The whole time they did not ask him was he okay or nothing. They just waited until medical showed up and they did not even run. They took their time while this guy had been laying on the floor for about 30 minutes. If it had been a CO they would have them off the floor and going to the hospital.

-Earl Gladding

Story 6:

Mental health....there is shitty follow up. Only trans seem to get the most or suicide attempts or if you're in a group. I've complained of elder abuse and all manner of things. Do you think there was an intervention or anything else? Do you think they checked on me? No. So we're basically on our own. So I check in when I can. I haven't even had a regular counselor for over 6 months. There is no cohesion between medical and psych either which would help greatly. They do just enough to look good on paper but in reality it just doesn't happen.

-Dana Gray

Story 7:

I, for one, have a lot to share in regards to my own mental wellness; both pre and post-incarceration. I did not come to prison addicted to drugs, I did not come from a broken home; my parents have been married for over 50 years. I was not abused as a child nor was I involved in gang activity. I've never owned a gun. All of the issues that usually lead individuals down the path to incarceration were absent in my life. I'm as "normal" as any member of your/our community. I worked my entire adult life, went to college, and had everything that a person my age and socioeconomic status could expect out of life. But with that being said, I was not mentally well. I was 40 years old, burned out by my job, going to WKU nearly full-time, in a difficult marriage, expecting a child, and having an extra-marital affair....talk about pressure. Most of my undoing was the result of self-inflicted wounds. I took on more responsibility than I could handle and ultimately snapped. The end of life as I knew it came to an abrupt halt one Saturday morning after a harsh verbal exchange with my wife. I ended up putting sleeping pills in her breakfast, waited until she went to sleep, and set fire to our home; knowing that she was asleep, and knowing full well that she may not have the opportunity to escape. By the grace of God, she was unharmed and minimal damage was done to our home. Our children were never in harm's way.

I have never denied what I did. I confessed to the investigators, and confessed my actions to my wife, my family and friends and sought help for what everyone knew as abnormal behavior. This was not the man that I was raised to be. Believe it or not, once everything came out into the open, my wife and I got help through marital counseling (both together and individually). She stayed with me knowing that I was completely stressed out and was not well mentally at the time. She, and her family, supported me during my trial, and wanted nothing more than for me to get the help that I needed and come home to my family. It wasn't all roses. They were very upset at what I did, but they knew it wasn't my normal behavior. My wife told the jurors that I was worth fixing.

I took my case to trial on the advice of

my attorney. We felt that I was being "overcharged" for what I did. My wife, along with her family, all testified for me during my trial; trying to paint a picture of a broken man who lost control of his mental stability. Their pleas were not enough. I received a 31-year prison sentence for what I did. I have done over 10 years of this time and still have 7 more years before I am parole eligible. Yes...I am guilty of what I did. I never denied that. I took the stand and told my jury what happened on that day. BUT...should an otherwise "normal" person be locked away for decades for something that could have been resolved with some good therapy and some probation? Not in KY. KY leads the nation in incarceration per capita, yet our crime rate has not decreased in the past 40 years. In fact, it has increased. Incarceration has not fixed the problem, yet it seems to be the first alternative to solve crime. Ironically, our state leaders all complain about the cost associated with incarceration, but none are willing to stick their necks out to advocate for any real changes. Most know that any politician who advocates for criminal reform will appear to be "soft on crime" in the public's eye. You need to look no further than our recent campaign ads to see how their stance on crime is used against each other during elections. What can be done? If the lawmakers are not willing to get in the game, then who can fix the broken system?

From a mental health standpoint (present day), I am well. I have a deeper appreciation for many of the things that you may take for granted. Just the other day, I was wondering what it would be like to eat with a metal fork. Crazy as it sounds...I have not eaten a meal with anything but a plastic spork for 10 years. I often wonder what it would be like to walk on carpet, or take a shower by myself (without shower shoes). A couple of years ago I was taken out for surgery (I had my gallbladder removed). I got sick on my way to the hospital because my eyes couldn't adjust to the speed of the vehicle. For the past 8 years, prior to my surgery, I had never gone faster than my legs could take me. There are many examples of the simple things that most wouldn't consider unless it was taken away. For months after I was incarcerated, I still kept reaching for my cell phone and would feel it vibrating on my leg. Obviously, it was gone, but the habit was still there. Today, I don't reach for my cell phone anymore, but there are still old habits that are hard to break.

For the record, my wife and I are no longer married. She divorced me after my conviction was affirmed by the Kentucky Supreme Court in 2014. She remarried shortly after and began a new life with her new husband. As a result, I have not seen our two children since our divorce in 2014. In short, most will tell you that they will be there through thick and thin. Most are out of your life after two or so years. It took my wife 2 years...most were gone well before that.

You stated that you wanted to learn more about the mental struggles associated with the loss of family and friends while locked up: Here is my perspective...fix a cup of coffee, this may get boring!

As I mentioned earlier, I took my case to trial. When the jury found me guilty, I was immediately taken into custody; I traded my suit and tie for my prison stripes. I spent the first 5-1/2 months in the county jail while I waited to be transferred to a processing facility. For the first couple of weeks while in the county, I would cover my head at night and cry myself to sleep...I tried to hide it from the men around me, not wanting to appear "soft". I missed holding my children, I missed my wife and the rest of my family. Fortunately, during these 5-1/2 months, I had visits from my family and was able to make phone calls to the people I knew...I was still in my community. Though I was in jail...I still felt like I was home, as crazy as it sounds. My family was only 15 minutes down the road. Most of the men in jail with me were from my hometown. Even if I didn't know them directly, I knew someone they knew, or vice-versa. I still felt somewhat connected to my hometown; things were familiar even though I was in an environment that was foreign to me. On the morning that I was shipped to the processing facility, I finally realized that I will not see my hometown for many, many years. As I was leaving, I just stared out the window....knowing that I was seeing it for the last time. It all started to sink in, that day. I didn't want to talk to the guys on transport with me, I just wanted to see everything for the last time.

Prison has hardened my heart. I don't think I am a cold hearted person. I'm not indifferent to loss or emotions. But, I have learned to deal with the pain of loss without sadness...does that make sense? I've had so much taken from me already, that loss is an expected way of life for me. When I walk out of prison, I will have nothing. Everything has been taken. I think if I lose my parents at this point I may not react the way I would have if I had been out there with the rest of the family. I think I would go about my day like normal. I hate that. I now have an "oh well"...attitude about loss or tragedy. In 10 years I have gone from everything hurting, not letting anything ever hurt me again. Is this good? Is this bad? It has its benefits. I'll let the world decide if it makes me a bad person or not. I still love and care for my family, I have empathy and compassion for others I just deal with things differently now.

-Anonymous Inmate

Story 8:

I've been CCCMS (normal care for mental illness) mental health patient for 18 years here in prison. In the past mental health hasn't always renewed my psychiatric meds. This has caused me to have breakdowns and end up in suicide watch in the past. I've also been treated sometimes with no compassion by mental health staff and by cops. All they do is provide medication with very little therapy. I've found my own therapy in arts and crafts.

-Lisa Lewis

Story 9:

I just wanted to share an experience I had in the Texas department of criminal justice system...I had been on medication for years for bipolar depression. When I went to prison, for drug possession, they asked my diagnosis for the meds. When I told her, she replied, "well while you're here, you're diagnosis is drug addiction and TDCJ does not medicate for drug addiction." And that's just one of many examples I could give....

-Terri Hooper

Story 10:

What is time? Time is when you're locked up in the system, for a determent amount of time away from as we say the world, I have done three rounds of time 4 yrs in California department of corrections, 14 years in the feds and 4 years in Texas, to me there are certain aspects of this time that have either gave me depression or PTSD. For example doors slamming, keys jingling, or certain words that are said that trigger certain actions, all caused by doing time, in terms its called being institutionalized, one thing we all go through is not letting the mind games that are played upon us as inmates or convicts, I feel the feds trip was the worst due to all the violence and having to be on your toes at all times because of all the culture from all over the world you are mixed up with.

I like to call it a bowl of cereal, because there is nothing but fruits, nuts and flakes all in a bowl. The administration and guards do their fair share of making inmates flip or pile on the mental games by treating as if you are not human. TDCJ is famous for that with their inhuman treatment of inmates and talking to you like you are a slave, picking cotton or as they say 4 stepping with a hoe.

Can a inmate claim PTSD? Good question, the whole incarceration aspect needs to be looked at as a whole because they are creating an institutionalized human through mental mind games and then want to hand out medication that causes more harm then good.

Did I take any meds for mental issues? No, I learned to deal with my surroundings and issues on my own, but with that said I paid for it today. I have done time in some of the worst prisons in this country, Leavenworth atl, Coleman Beaumont Elreno, Folsom, Chino, just to name a few. I am a product of Americans war on drugs. I have been home now for two years and work in an industry that I don't have to deal with people, which is wastewater, and I have a little business dealing with inmates in Texas with parole.

I see more women who have mental issues in Texas and deal with it through medication, then I do men, and maybe that's the way folks decide to deal with their mental illness. So in closing, I feel there is a major problem with mental illness within the system that is pushed out the door onto the world, that is caused by the system as a whole, how do we fix that? Get these men and women the help they need to deal with their issues and make prison a place where you can live without fighting your own demons caused by the corruption of the system

-David Cummings

Story 11:

As far as my experience with mental health in prison. I just don't know what to say. They have psych prisons here in Texas where they will send you if you hurt yourself or threaten to where people are eating their own shit and smearing it all over their bodies. So anything that I've seen or experienced is nothing to that.

I do not see a therapist...however I seem to be using you as one. I often wonder why I let you into my head. It helps me though...its nice to have someone I can talk to about this stuff. It really does and I thank you for that. Nobody else has ever wanted to hear this stuff.

I am on medication. They're for my anxiety and I don't know what they call it but I tell them I can't even look at some of the people in here because they make me sick to my stomach...I fucking hate them so much I can hardly breathe. It's the truth! I can be very judgmental with high standards and theirs some real trash in here.

As far as mental health in prison goes I'm much more healthy in here then I was in the

world. It's been a good experience. I tell them
what's wrong and they give me meds. I can be
completely insane and no one cares. I have my
own cell and they feed me 3 times a day. They
even give me clean laundry and shit. In the
world if you're having mental problems it shows
and you suffer for it, in here, it's no big deal...it
doesn't matter. That being said they're different
kinds of mental problems. Some people aren't
doing so good. I seem to hide my demons well
enough...most of the time anyway.

-Anonymous Inmate

Story 12:

I don't really know where to start so I will just speak on what really messed me up mentally! So basically the prison I was at before this one was called Warren Correctional Institution and I was treated very poorly down there and with huge prejudice. I don't know if you know but the reason I am serving 24 years is for an aggravated robbery and felonious assault against a correctional officer. In 2017, I made the mistake of robbing and shooting a guy in the stomach who later flat lined but was revived and come to find out he was a CO aka prison guard so I think that's why they gave me so much time.

Anyways when I got to Warren I was told multiple times by their staff and administration that because of my crime and what I did to a fellow officer they would make my time as hard as possible and since then my time being incarcerated there I was beaten and maced while in handcuffs for no reason. I was thrown in blocks with rival gangs purposely. There were times when I was in the hole and I was denied food or just downright scared to eat because of all the threats I received.

There were also times when I was called racial slurs by guards and I was constantly verbally, physically and mentally abused everyday. There were some points where I thought I couldn't take it anymore and sometimes I still feel like that to this day because of all the trauma all this has caused me. This is why I am now taking it upon myself to start reaching out to the world just for some mental support because you would be surprised just how much a little bit of encouragement means or how good it feels to know I'm not going through this alone! Prison is a tough place and a tough environment and you can't cry in here or show any weakness or everyone will take that and run with it so I'm just trying to get by day by day!

-Darshoned Jackson

Story 13:

My friend said she was suicidal and mental health sent her back and wouldn't take her. She went back to her room and tried to slit her writs and cops pepper sprayed her in her room. She is close to 70 years old with a walker. They took her to a cage and sent her to crisis and then brought her back to the same room. She was catatonic again in here and our staff saw she needed mental health and they took her and kept her. This is common practice in here.

-Anonymous Inmate

Story 14:

Along with a string of very bad decisions my mental health is the reason I'm here. I tried to get help before all the crazy shit happened but I was told nothing that was going on with me was serious enough to worry about. Just my self medication by itself was enough to tear lives apart.

So right now I'm on three different medications for my mental health. It's taken a while to find the right combo that works but I think I'm there right now. My head is clear and not overwhelmed by my own thoughts. In terms of meds, I'm good. Counseling is a different thing. Anything I say to a mental health counselor here can and will be used against me in a disciplinary fashion. I've seen it happen to a lot of guys. So, I just don't talk to them about anything they can use. They are not here to help me, that's for damn sure.

-Anonymous Inmate

Story 15:

I worked at a major prison in Kansas for a year after I had retired. I worked in the Mental Health Department at the prison, had direct involvement with the inmates and led a PTSD support group during that time.

The Mental Health Department had a major role in supporting the inmates mental health and safety. Each inmate was checked several times per shift to assess their mental health, physical condition and concerns. Records of each interaction were kept so any changes of behavior could be tracked and interventions taken.

The Mental Health Department worked very closely with the medical part of the prison, for medications, changes in inmate behaviors, health concerns and most importantly for mental conditions that would lead to any suicidal behaviors, including starvation protests, aging issues and major mental health issues that would present dangerously for the inmate or the prison environment.

Overall, inmates at this prison were very well taken care of, both mentally and physically.

They had options to participate in art therapy, GED and educational programs, sports and gym time, numerous support groups, individual therapy, dog training programs, obtaining jobs within the prison, and prison community activities, such as art shows, music programs, etc.

Although things can always be improved, I believe that the inmates were well taken care if they would allow for the assistance provided, or tried to become involved in programs that would assist them in finding a positive outlook for their future.

-L.C., PhD

Story 16:

What is mental illness to me? Nothing to me! To know is much better than thinking...thoughts, is neither spirit nor matter; the mental mind isn't neither either of me; the absolute is way beyond the mind; the mind cannot understand it, therefore, we have to intuitively over-stand, and understand its true divine nature inside all of us; but all is not able to over-stand where I'm from Mr. Bruce; the absolute is beyond conditioned.

Life here on this plane; it is beyond that which is relative. It is the real being; It is non-being because it does not keep any concordance with our concepts. So when you speak on the mentally illness of people; I cannot myself entertain delusion's humanity mind plays this delusional game of life with each other sir, Mr. Bruce; the absolute is the real being of all beings. This is why most people in this delusional world cannot comprehend it, to be is better than to exist.

Mental illness is very real. This is a mental health prison, I've experienced being around the mentally ill, its basically where I grew up at, poor areas. Broken homes, abandonment, rape victims, most I've spoken to over these years. They're victims of child molestation and raped by their own family members.

It all starts at home. We all came from different worlds, everyone didn't grow up in a middle class home with a golden or silver spoon in their mouths. When a child is victimized by their own parents and family members, and bullied most of their lives in school, hated and discriminated and misjudged by a bias racist society these kids do not feel welcomed and accepted as equals, of course it can grow into a mental issue and lead up to mental illness for anyone of any tribe.

People mainly become mentally deranged by other people mental health problems. Other people's mental health most times can make others mentally ill, its like they say. Birds with feathers flock together. Meaning; if you hang around a bunch of negativity, you will end up negative, if you flock with deranged people. You will end up a dangerous person. Its all about how people were first bred and raised up around.

Most likely you'll end up like the bad bunch,
that's if you grew up around a bunch of rotten
apples majority of your life. Its like I've said Mr.
Bruce. It all starts at home. That's the beginning
how most people of today ended up mentally ill.
That's the noble truth.

-Howard Belcher

Story 17:

So my first time I ever dealt with mental health I was eighteen years old and I just threw hot water on a child molesters face and because he was a child molester they done a standard interview asking if I had childhood abuse issues. While I was in seg they came to see me a few times but when they realized I did it because he was a child molester they stopped visiting. From my first experience with them they did seem to care.

My second experience came on my third time in prison because a celly I had tried to hang himself. He was heavily medicated and would visit the mental health office twice a week. They had him on so much medication he would sleep 20 hours a day. For 2 days in a row he tried getting the block officer to call mental health and he kept saying they were coming. After the investigation we found out he never called. My celly didn't die but I never saw him again. They interviewed me and seemed genuinely pissed off they weren't called and the correctional officer was fired.

The last time I dealt with mental health in

Massachusetts I was having pain and ended up finding out I had a kidney stone. After going to the hospital, the standard procedure is you spend 3-5 days in the medical/mental health ward. I seen some really crazy things while there. They had these cells that had just bars, so if a correctional officer was a jerk, there were guys so crazy they would throw piss and shit at them. There was one so crazy they had him strapped down all the time and when they brought him out to shower 2 officers had to bring him and he wore a spit guard at all times. He was very nuts. I also seen 2 guys they called cutters and one of them had scars all over his arms from cutting himself.

The other guy I never seen really but I remember the nurses got called to his cell when he cut himself. This block was so bad they had one nurse and one mental health worker there 24 hours a day. Even in that short time there I seen the nurse one time get knocked out, right in front of me, it was scary to be honest. I guess this guy kept telling her he was in pain and his stomach was hurting bad. She kept giving him Motrin, its the prison medicals go to thing, Ibuprofen came the next night and he got rushed to the hospital from seg because he had appendicitis and his appendix had burst. Prison medical is horrible most of the time, I've seen many bad care stories in my life.

So my next experience was when I was arrested for the current charge of felony murder. During the entry interview with the mental health staff they asked if I was depressed and felt like hurting myself. I was just arrested, and I was honest, I said hell yeah I'm depressed and who knows if I'd hurt myself? It was the wrong thing to say because for the next 48 hours I was put in a room and was under 24/7 watch. All they gave me was a Ferguson suit which I hated so I literally walked around naked, and slept naked. I kept telling the mental health staff I was okay and was getting so pissed I even started doing naked jumping jacks, which don't do because it hurt, balls need to be constrained during jumping jacks.

So I finally convinced them I was sane after a mental health doctor sat with me and asked me many questions. It was one of the most humiliating times and I promised myself to never say the wrong thing to the mental health staff.

So the next time I dealt with mental health staff it was the worst day of my life. I was called to the captains office and when I got there, there was 2 correctional officers, the captain and a mental health counselor and the priest.

They were informing me that my son had passed and I lost it. So the priest and mental health counselor talked to me for a few and they let me call my family and the counselor arranged for a special visit with my cousins, sister and father to come see me. So in this instance they really looked out and helped me. She even came to check on me for a week or so every couple of days. So no complaints on this instance.

The last instance I remember dealing with mental health is when I was diagnosed with leukemia. They did a standard interview and made sure I wasn't depressed and was going to hurt myself. So after they determined I was okay they left me alone. That actually wasn't the last instance, my father passed away a year later from Alzheimer. It was actually a mental health counselor who helped me set up special visits so I'd be able to see him in a private room. They really looked out and when he passed away they made sure I was okay and let me make some calls. She even offered me some antidepressants if I was feeling depressed from the losses. I didn't accept though because I don't like the side effects, they make you feel all tired and out of it, had many cellies who are on them including my current celly Joseph Rizzo. I see first hand how these meds they give these guys are so powerful but in most cases it seems to be helping.

So now I have a few stories of instances I've seen personally. The first I remember I was transferred to a different prison than the one I'm in now. I'm currently in MacDougall Walker Correctional Institution and was transferred out of the blue to Cheshire Prison. When there I had 2 cellies who were heavily sedated. The first was an older man who thought everyone was out to get him including me. He carried a shank on him everywhere and one day he comes in the cell and said if the food servers don't give him an extra tray and only gives them to their boys, he was going to stab them. I even know he saw the mental health counselor that day and he told me he told her the same thing. Guess they didn't believe him. Anyways that night he asked for an extra tray and I sat next to the area where they pass the food out. When I heard them tell him no I shook my head but honestly I didn't think he would do it...well right then he pulled out his shank and stabbed one in the neck and the other in the stomach. They fought back but the correctional officers responded fairly quick. There was blood everywhere.

Well that night the lieutenant and mental health counselor called me to her office and asked me a bunch of questions, like did you know he would do this? Or did you know he had a shank? I said I had no clue and he told me he told you and I pointed at the counselor. The lieutenant seem surprised and I heard later she got into trouble. I feel from my experience they don't take guys seriously, they just give them pills and say you will be okay.

The last incident worth mentioning was when I was brought to Massachusetts from Connecticut to take care of my cases there, I spent nine weeks in Massachusetts State Prison,

Walpole. Its where they put the worst of the worst. Because I was from out of state they put me in a special block that housed guys that were waiting to be moved to other prisons, since I was being moved to Connecticut once my cases were closed. Well there was a guy who was a tier man and he swept the day room everyday. They called him mental. Yep, that was his nickname, but I guess he's earned it over the years. Well I guess he was sorta well known and dealt with mental health a lot. I knew because I found out he was from my hometown city (Worcester, Massachusetts) So I talked to him and we were cool and knew some of the same people and a lot of the places in the city. Anyways, he told me about all the medications they had him on and I soon realized he was mental.

In the morning and afternoon he was a funny outgoing man. At night he was a walking zombie and if I called him he wouldn't be able to comprehend anything. One morning after being warned repeatedly a lieutenant showed up to fire him for being late. Well he flipped out, took all of his clothes off and threatened to stab himself in the ass with a broomstick if they didn't give him his job back. I'm dead serious. He didn't and they shot him with mace and brought him to the hole. So there was a case of over medicated for sure.

-Christopher Peltier

Story 18:

DREAMTIME

I should like to talk to Sigmund Freud and the prophet Daniel about my dreams...

Depending on how you use the word "dream", this environment either promotes them as sustenance that you rely on to keep from starving, or smothers them like concrete poured over grass. You dream like a man in a straightjacket dreams of moving his arms, like a thirsty man dreams of cool water, like a pregnant woman dreams of a healthy child. Sometimes you dream of schemes and different paths because all you have left to explore is in your mind. Our dreams, in all the senses of the word, change over time. Perhaps they improve, perhaps they become more terrible, but they always become influenced by your environment.

I spent a year recording my dreams, about eight years into my sentence. You know those moments when you wake up and recall a particularly vivid dream and want to remember it but want to roll over and fall back asleep just a little more? I forced myself to grab a piece of paper and pen that I kept on the radiator just below my bunk scribbled notes on every single dream I had for an entire year. Shadows of people I had known and life-like ones I had imagined combined in places that I recognized but were different, as though the universal law of change even applies to our unconscious. The pond I used to spend so much time on and around as a kid developed a razor-wire topped fence surrounding it, yet still I loved lounging there. People I knew and used to know kept me company, lovers embraced me. It was 2013, I'd been locked up since 2005, and the earliest I can get out of prison is the year 2030. I would get through my days sometimes just to sleep.

[Out of that time came some of the writing and poems that I am most proud of, as well as a better understanding of myself.]

During the daytime, I dreamed of more and was not able to achieve it, barred from the resources necessary to do so... this being the very nature of prison. Incapacitated, I sunk into my beige existence. I lost much of a sense of self, clinging to what little I had, living vicariously through others, looking for distractions or anything that reminded me of color. My life meant little to me, but I wanted it to mean more. I felt like I meant little to others, even when I did matter. Eastern religions and philosophies emphasize living within the moment, but one is assumed to go into these moments with a sense of spirit. I was alive, but my soul was not. When I was awake, my soul was asleep.

The men I live around dream as well, and minds are incarcerated by more than just physical walls. Dreams hampered by feelings of inadequacy, dreams of the easy way, dreams of success by cleverness or ferocity instead of discipline. Some dream of other's worst dreams coming true. Some forget their dreams after decades, and some no longer dream at all.

Sometimes I'd sleep too much, but I never stopped dreaming. My literal dreams at night took on aspects of my environment, like fences and officers and count-times, but despite my earning my prison sentence, I never dreamed myself as merely a prisoner. Even in my darkest personal times, I dreamed that I could do something more. I dreamed that I could be something more.

Broken dreams and nightmares from all those touched by, or involved in, the criminal justice system are the foundations that prisons are built on. But I don't want this to become all that I am, or all that I ever was. And so in my waking days, I started to pay more attention to the little things around me, the little moments in my life that were special. I found the spirit of the day again, and the spirit in my life again. I was able to take more control of my dreams because I accept my life as it is, as I've made it, and take that as a starting place for new things. By focusing my dreams, I find that more of them come true. I am happier, and more at peace, while also able to do more for others. I write better, I've learned to write and play beautiful music. I read and study on and learn so many subjects I never had before. I'm a student of horticulture, mycology, religion, architecture, law, music, and economics. I couldn't dream of more with what I had, so I decided to dream of more in other ways. And my dreams at night take me to new places despite not having walked outside of prison for over half of my life.

Dreams fade, and die at day, and then you sleep and dream anew. It's one thing that can never be taken from me.

-Christopher Dankovich

Story 19:

There are times in our lives that we don't want to admit we have problems dealing with life. My name is Chander and when I committed my crimes, I myself was in terror. Questions ran through my head...What the???...How???... even more, WHY? As a young man of 20 not understanding how I just ended the lives of three people just sent me into a darker abyss of my own making. My story is not about the abyss but how I climbed my way out.

After my crime and sitting in a jail cell, I'm told by my lawyers not to say anything to anyone about my case. The fear of what I did and thinking am I what the media is calling me? Doubt in yourself and others goes away very fast. Don't trust the jail mental health people I'm told. For very good reason, because one even testified for the prosecution in my case. I'm sentenced to "Life in prison without the possibility of parole" under what was the "Three Strikes Law". Ask yourself how would you feel? The emotional rage that was in me at the time of my crimes is still there. Boiling and could resurface again. Not knowing if I'm really mentally insane or just an evil person. If I wasn't already damaged, I guess I am now.

The first nine years of my incarceration were spent in the depression of my own rage and anger. Conflicts with myself and others, hateful towards the world for what my life had become. None of this was what I imagined my life would have been. Of all my friends and loved ones only my parents and younger brother stood by to support me. Consumed in guilt and shame the only thing I allowed them to do was support me financially. Of course I had psychologists and psychiatrists come speak to me and ask how I was doing? How are you supposed to be doing when there is no trust in anyone, feelings of betrayal, fear that others can hear your thoughts. Fear of ones own self is perhaps the greatest mental illness.

In 1999, I was transferred to one of Virginia's state of the art super Max state prisons, Red Onion State Prison. This prison would have put so much distance between my family and myself. Losing contact with those that you love can leave one hopeless and with despair in life.

My family called and requested the help of the psychiatrist that was treating me at my previous institution. That doctor made so many calls on my behalf and had me transferred back within nine days. How many people can convince the department of corrections that they made a mistake. It was then that my tearful younger brother said to me, "You don't talk to us about what happened, and your doctor said you don't really talk to him. Please open up to him and let him help you, he's a good doctor. " I promised him that I would. That began a series of conversations between myself and my psychiatrist. Healing doesn't come easy, after experiencing childhood trauma, college hazing and quietly dealing with depression, it takes years.

During my trial I was diagnosed and told that I suffered from paranoid schizophrenia. Over several years of therapy I believe a correct diagnosis was given to me, what I was told was, PTSD (Post-Traumatic Stress Disorder). Of course PTSD was not an available diagnose in 1990, so l learned many things about myself, my wrongful thinking and internal anger that was bottled up for years. This process took all of fifteen years if not more. Like I said, Mental Health recovery isn't over night and it can be very emotional coming to terms of your own hurt. Learning this put me in a better place to help others around me.

In society and especially prison, mental health treatment can carry a negative stigma. Being open about treatment can help others to also seek counseling. Of course you will always have your share of psychologist and psychiatrist that truly care and those that are just happy to have a state job. I got lucky I guess, the good Lord blessed me with people that wanted the best for me, even when I wouldn't open up. They kept knocking on the door, never quitting. There were times during treatment that I wanted to quit, but they let me have my time outs and helped me regroup. As I said, I got lucky.

Because many of my peers saw my growth over the years, I was asked to become a mentor in an offender lead program called Second Chance Quest. I took over sessions dealing with personal growth and maturity among young men. Of course I spoke about all my problems in sessions, by doing this I gained the respect and understanding of many of our participants. This also allowed them to share their experience and find ways to repair their past conditionings.

A few years later a friend and I started a parole support group to help older offenders cope with constant denials from the parole board. This group grew into something more by the second year. We were not only sharing the pains of our parole turn downs, but we began to discuss victim awareness and the trauma we caused others.

Hey, you gotta deal with your past in order to move forward. It's not easy looking at the harm we caused other people, it takes strength to look that person you once were and put that person to rest. Many of the guys I see get involved with drugs and alcohol can't cope with what they did in their crimes.

I came to a realization a few years back. I took the lives of three people, I left their bodies out in the open to be discovered. They never ever left me, I feel that my victims were the ones that wanted answers for my actions. They didn't hurt me, they guided me to solutions and recovery. I owed them that much.

Some may not understand what I am about to say but people should know that the universe does have a plan. Recovery can not happen without having some faith or a religion to follow. A book called "House of Healing", by Robin Casarjian, there is an excellent chapter about what forgiveness is and is not. Saying that you are forgiven because of a righteous attitude saying, " I forgive myself because God has forgiven me ---when, in truth, you haven't done the inner work and soul searching that is necessary for healing. This isn't real forgiveness people, its a cop-out. Feeling connected to a faith or spirituality should give you the strength and power of unconditional love to overcome any demons that you fight with every day. Demons such as: drugs, alcohol, porn, rage, hate and any thing else we battle with.

I have to shamelessly say my faith journey was a very long process, remember I said recovery isn't easy or quick. A close friend, David suggested I start doing Siddha Yoga lessons. Yoga??? Really??? Yoga can mean a lot of things, but the root of yoga is to go within one's self. Isn't that what Jesus did in the desert? So I would get these meditation lessons monthly and contemplate on what I read. This helped me to find a calmness in myself so that I could look at why I was so messed up. Knowing half your problems is the solution. How many people do you know that say, "There's nothing wrong with me."

I tried going to the many church services offered in prison. Found them to be fake and not offering me anything. Looking back, that was a very selfish way to think. The Yoga lessons took time to sink in, almost eleven years before I tried church again. An old girlfriend of mine came back into my life, we would often speak about faith. Often times she would question her own faith and what she believed. I went and tried church again, thinking I would learn something to help her. As many of you know maintaining relationships in prison is difficult, she stopped speaking with me nine months after I started finding myself in a new faith. No, I'm not upset with her, maybe getting me back into faith was her purpose. Well, I stuck going to church and that power of unconditional love helped me in my last phase of recovery. I've been involved with a religious way of life for six years now and going strong. Having a sense of faith really helped me stay afloat during one of the worst times in our time period. Many people took the wrong paths during the Covid-19 pandemic. I feel blessed that the Lord guided me and kept me on a clear and clean path. During the pandemic lockdown many of the offenders I knew here turned to alcohol and drugs. During the pandemic, we lost five men to Covid-19, and seven to drug overdoses. Sad, but a reality.

Going back to programming, a co-worker and someone I consider a friend asked me to help him create a new group. This group was intended to help many offenders cope with parole denials year after year. I asked my buddy, "Calvin, what do we even know about parole denials? We're not even parole eligible." Diving head first and letting God lead the way we formed, "The Parole Peer Group ". This group was not learning how to make parole, but learning how to understand our hurt of these denials from the parole board. After serving many years incarcerated, individuals can sometimes become disconnected as to why they are locked up. They remember their charges, but they forget their crimes. Watching videos of victims speak about the crimes committed against them or their loved ones was difficult for many of us. There were a few guys that would tell me that I was just trying to make them feel guilty. Some guys would quit but many followed through feeling the pain they caused others. I think knowing that pain can help to become a person that would never commit such acts again.

Remember when I said that I had been sentenced to Life without possibility of parole because of the "Three Strikes Law"? Guess what??? Some how, some reason the good Lord saw to it that I have parole hearings. In 2018, the Three Strikes Law was overturned in The Commonwealth of Virginia. After 32 years I was now eligible for a parole hearing. God is good. After my first hearing I was denied in 28 days with four reasons that are beyond my control. (Note: When I say beyond my control, many of the reasons to turn a individual down for parole are beyond our controls. How can we change things from the past.) Along with this the parole board at that time determined not to grant me another hearing for three years. Yes, all this after serving 32 years under a law that was determined to be unconstitutional. Politicians, right??? Of course I was devastated, but used what I learned to keep myself out of depression.

That weekend I guess I did a Forest Gump thing. I started my normal two mile run and just kept going. Running around and around on the prison yard track letting go of all the hurt and pain I felt. Oh, if I forgot this was in the first week of July. I hadn't shared my denial with anyone yet. My buddy, Calvin, was sitting at a table and asked how much was I going to run and said get some water. He could tell I was hurting from the run and something else. I told him about the parole turn down and we talked. He let me know that I need to let others in my circle know so they can support me.

Surprisingly, a few staff members honestly showed concern and disappointment in the parole hearing also. Knowing that there were people that believed in me, gave me greater reason to pick myself up and move forward.

People, stop crying about what you don't have be thankful what you do have. Sure, I wish many of my old friends believed in me, but I'm so grateful for those that I do have.

Being thankful, you wouldn't understand. I had two scholarships when I went to college. I blew them but then something to be thankful for, I was selected to be a part of the University of Virginia, Darden School of Business and a group called Resilience Education pilot program here at Buckingham C. C. This program was initially only done at Fluvanna Correctional Center for Women, mainly for women that were victims of domestic violence. The data that was compiled had shown that 60% of the offenders at Fluvanna C.C. were victims of domestic violence and lacked the knowledge of financial independence. Financial literacy is a major issue for individuals that are at highest risk of vulnerability. It has now been expanded to include B.K.C.C and another facility.

Remember I told you that the very three that I hurt were pushing me to be better. I've been able to gain a lot of knowledge in just the first phase of the program, Financial

Capabilities. Still have Entrepreneurship and Foundations in Business to complete. This program helped me to see a red flag financial patterns in my own life that led me to my crimes.

In 1990, we did not get red flag warnings on cell phones. Looking at those pattern gives me better understanding of my failures. Furthermore, looking at the reasons for past failures are lessons learned to better stability. A lack of financial stability can lead to a decline in mental health. Just learning to be aware of signs helps in recovery.

This May 30th I will again start a new process for a parole hearing. Hoping and praying that the parole board members can see the change in me from when I committed my crimes. I would like to ask you, can you see the process and hard work for change? If you can I hope this would inspire you to also begin a change in yourself. As humans we are always hurting and healing, I see society today and ask why have we fallen so low. I can not bare to see another school shooting. When do we as a community reach into our schools and ask our children, how do they really feel. I wish someone I trusted asked me that in 1990. Truthfully, a friend did ask once, I wish I had called Debby that day just to talk and let her know my hurt. Don't be afraid if your child speaks about their hurt, it takes a brave person to speak it openly. This took me many years to understand.

I am always looking for new friends to be a part of a support circle, you may contact me through JPay.com Chander Matta #1171204 Buckingham Correctional Center, Dillwyn, Va.

I would like to thank the many people that were a part of my recovery. Also, thanks to Mr. LeMaster for this opportunity and Mr. Dodge for recommending me.

Thank you for believing not only in me but in second chances. Peace!

-Chander Matta

Story 20:

When I was first arrested for defending myself from a drunken convicted felon with a gun that the serial number had been scratched out, and charged with murder I was suicidal depressed. Because 1) I took another human beings life, despite the FACT that I was going to die if I had not inadvertently caused his death. 2) The cop that never mirandized me lied to the news media to cover up this FACT.

So when I tried to explain the problem it seemed like they were evaluating my obviously ridiculous story in an effort to get me to admit I had murdered this drug dealer because he was black.

"If you were not read your Miranda Rights you would not be here."

"If he was he ordered to leave and came back with a gun you wouldn't be here."

"Your suicidal thoughts will go away once you admit to yourself and the police that you would not have killed that man with the 8 month old daughter."

Now, all of the recordings have been destroyed so I have no physical evidence off

these interrogations by the mental health staff
Garner or Walker. There was NO mental health
staff at Northern level 5 maximum prison. There
is more but I don't like to say things without
evidence to back me up.

All I know is when I showed the head
psychologist the physical evidence she said "you
can't blame us for not believing you, I've never
seen this amount of legal misrepresentation
before." Let that speak for itself, my mental
health status is now a 2. Five is the worst. 1 is
the best. I don't believe the mental health staff
cared one bit about my depression or if I killed
myself. In a nutshell that's it.

I can't explain it without showing you the
doctor's report to the judge, which was
completely false. It wasn't even my report. I am
allergic to opium base painkillers. But nobody
said anything about it because I'm a long-haired
white guy from Florida who killed a black guy.
End of line.

-Jeffrey Hall

Story 21:

The system is broken. There is no actual help for someone with mental illness in the penal system. I am a supervising level correctional officer at a maximum security prison so when I say the system is broken you best believe it. I have worked every level from community corrections up to maximum security and have seen so many inmates that didn't need prison, they needed help with mental illness.

I won't disclose the state or facility that I work for nor will I tell you my name. Do you want to know how mental health in the prison deals with someone who is struggling enough to try and take their own life? They put them in a suicide smock with no socks or underwear and give them a mattress with no blankets and then they are alone in a cell with the lights on and an officer outside outside the door either checking on them every 15 minutes or constantly watching them.

They get a paper bag with bread, peanut butter and an apple to eat. If for any reason the door to the cell needs opened they have to be cuffed and have 2 officers present to accompany the medical staff inside the cell. I don't know about you but if I'm emotionally spent to the point I try and take my own life being put in that situation would not help me one bit. Mental health checks in once a day afterwards to slowly allow the inmate to have socks or upgrade their watch to 30 or 60 minutes.

They then give them meds and tell them it will help. There is no therapy or treatment other than meds. If the inmate doesn't want to take the meds they can then have a hearing to force medicate the said inmate. Even then, what help is that? There has to be an alternative. So many of these people don't have families and are institutionalized at this point. Most will never go on to be rehabilitated and part of society. It is a vicious cycle that needs a solution.

Mental illness is a big part of why people turn to drugs or commit crimes. Until the root of the problem is found and treated there will be no change. It's not just in the penal system, it's on every corner in every city. Most correctional facilities are low staffed on officers as well as medical staff which only makes it that much harder for inmates that need help. The caseload is huge and burnout is a real thing.

Does that make it okay? No, but this country is in a mental health crisis with no end in sight. When a grown man is naked and painting the walls with feces singing one minute and fully dressed having a normal conversation with someone the next and has been for months then whatever mental health is doing isn't working. I know there are people out there that don't care because they're inmates but they are human beings that deserve basic human rights. I'll say it once more for those in the back, THE SYSTEM IS BROKEN!

-Anonymous correctional officer

Cook County Sheriff's Office Mental Health Programs Summary:

Cook County Sheriff's Office Crisis Intervention Training

➢ According to the Cook County Sheriff's website, on any given day, between 25-30 percent of the individuals in custody at Cook County Jail suffer from mental illnesses.

➢ The Sheriff's Office made Crisis Intervention Training (CIT) mandatory for all police in 2016. The 40-hour training includes how to respond, react, and assist those who are in a state of mental health crisis and emphasizes de-escalation. o All members of the police department are CIT trained.

➢ Since 2013, all new Department of Corrections recruits receive 40 hours of CIT and veterans are also receiving training.
-Recruits receive a total 80-hours of mental health training.

-Our mandate goes above and beyond state law which requires 40 hours of CIT for police officers.

Treatment Response Team - Co-Responder Virtual Program

➢ While Crisis Intervention Training is extremely important, it is merely the first step in our mental health assistance. The Cook County Sheriff's Office has, for years, worked to assist those in crisis while in custody through mental health programming with the hopes of ending their interaction with the criminal justice system and bettering their futures as they re-enter their communities.

➢ The Treatment Response Team (TRT) Co-Responder Virtual Assistance Program (CVAP) assists those in need of mental health or crisis intervention through the use of an electronic tablet.

-This unit gives Sheriff's Police, and anyone they meet, 24/7 access to a clinician virtually via tablet or phone. They help deescalate situations in real time and, importantly, follow-up with individuals and their families to help them identify and stick with treatment plans.

       -Since the creation of CVAP in 2021, it has expanded to 14 suburbs and now covers more than 500,000 residents in unincorporated Cook County and municipalities.

➢This program ultimately helps public safety in a few ways:

       -Allows Police to clear a scene in which public safety is not an issue.

       -Gives an individual in crisis or their loves ones another avenue for assistance than having to call 9-1-1 for a police response.

       -With case management provided by CVAP clinicians, the underlying concerns that have caused individuals to call police are addressed.

Community Resource Center

➢Launched in September 2020 to address the impending evictions crisis and the continued growing need for mental health, substance abuse, and other social service assistance.

-The Community Resource Center (CRC) built a database of governmental/non-profit social service agencies with a broad array of assistance.

-CRC staff can directly connect individuals to community-based agencies that can address their needs. Also helps connect discharging detainees to services.

-CRC is staffed with expertise in mental health, substance abuse issues, trauma-informed care, and knowledge of other branches of the Sheriff's Office – such as the CCDOC, Electronic Monitoring, Treatment Response Team, and Social Services Evictions Support Unit – coordinate provision of seamless care to participants.

Mental Health Jail Programming

➤ The Jail operates or hosts dozens of programs, and while some of them are expressly intended to address participant's mental health issues, the reality is that there is some mental health component to virtually every program.

➤ The Office has 13 licensed clinicians/counselors on staff who help run programs in the jail. (Licensed counselors, licensed social workers, etc.)

➤ Staff employ the Individualized Assessment and Strategic Assignment (IASA), a framework developed by the Sheriff's Office to identify appropriate programming and resources both inside and outside the jail for each person in custody.

➤ Started in August 2014, the Mental Health Transition Center (MHTC) is a voluntary program that uses group counseling and cognitive behavior therapies to help participants identify and address issues that led to criminal justice system involvement. First of its kind in the country, it provides comprehensive treatment, life skills, education, and discharge planning for inmates with mental health issues/diagnoses.

➢ The Sheriff's Anti-Violence Effort (SAVE) was created in 2016 to reach an extremely high-risk group of 18-24-year-olds from Chicago's most violent plagued communities.

Substance Use Assistance Programs

➢ Therapeutic Healing Recovery Initiative for Vitality & Empowerment (THRIVE) is a women's substance abuse program in the Jail. This court-ordered program seeks to target those struggling with substance use issues and equip them with the support and tools they need to be successful in the community.

➢ Sheriffs Men's Addiction Recovery Treatment (SMART) is the men's substance abuse program in the Jail. Our program is holistic and addressed the biopsychological needs of the participants. This program uses cognitive behavioral therapy to identify how substance use is impacting one's life and learn skills to reduce the likelihood of using substances to self-medicate their underlying issues.

➢ Sheriffs Opioid Addiction Recovery (SOAR) is a program that identifies individuals in the Jail with opioid use disorders. We engage in individuals and offer in custody programs and services and advocate with the Public Defender, State's Attorney's Office, and Judiciary to transition the individual to Electronic Monitoring with intense case management services to help with their transition to the community during such a vulnerable time frame.

-Cook County Sheriff's Office

Norway Prison Better?:

The cells have a bed, a small fridge, a bookshelf, TV, desk and a chair, plus a private bathroom including a shower, toilet and a sink. In the school building there is also a grocery store named "Justisen" (The Justice) where inmates can buy whatever they need to cook for themselves and each other. There is also a well equipped music studio – "Criminal Records", a garden, a holy room, a gym, training room, library, computer room, family visiting house and more. The school offers prisoners an opportunity to get a proper education while serving their sentence.

During the day guards often socialize with the prisoners. It could be over waffles and coffee, dinner, volleyball or just casual conversations. Many areas have no surveillance cameras, and prisoners can to some extent move around freely. Many have suggested the prison is too luxurious, that being in a prison like this is not a proper punishment. Warden Are Høidal says that revenge alone does not provide any good results. Rehabilitation is key. Finding proper housing and a steady income even before the prisoners are released is believed to contribute to lower recidivism rates.

I'm sure most of you will read that and say that isn't prison. What if I told you Norway has one of the lowest recidivism rates in the whole world. In 2016, only 20% of inmates re-offend within a few years after being released. The United States is on the higher end of around 75%-76%.

Norway's prison system is considered very effective in what it does. The maximum sentence you can receive is 21 years (30 for crimes against another person and only life for military related crimes). It doesn't stop at 21 years though because at the end of the sentence the prison can add another 5 years to the prisoner's sentence if they are deemed not rehabilitated.

The guards are referred to officers and are trained in communication. It's almost like they're role models, coaches, or even mentors to some of the prisoners. It can take up to 2 to 3 years to complete the training. One study I found interesting is the life expectancy of an American correctional officer is just 59 years old compared to the national average of 75 years old.

    "Norway's official policy is to produce a person who, "when the sentence has been served, is drug-free or in control of his drug use, has a suitable place to live, can read, write and do math, has a chance on the job market, can relate to family and friends and society at large, are able to seek help for problems that may arise after release and can live independently."

    This will probably cause an uproar because it comes down to taxpayers making things better for prisoners because Norway spends roughly $93,000 each year per prisoner in its system. From everything I had read it is effective, but as you can see it's not cheap. You know how much United States spends on prisoners? $31,000 per year. I bet 9 out of 10 times I could ask someone living in United States about spending more money to improve living conditions for criminals and their answer would be hell no!

    I'm no expert in this field and shouldn't be viewed as one, but talking to a lot of these criminals for the past 10 years, I can tell you this...most of them never had a chance in life and this would allow them another chance with proper education and skills to succeed in the real world plus give them routes on where to ask for help if a problem surfaced for them. Most prisoners that are released in the United States just re-offends because they come back out on the streets to struggle again just like they did before they were locked up. There is a change to be made, but most individuals aren't going to care to make that change sadly because in most people's eyes that I know will say "they done the crime so pay the time."

Sources:
-https://www.thestoryinstitute.com/halden
-https://medium.com/wagovernor/how-norwegian-prisons-prepare-inmates-to-become-better-neighbors-534409a90f33
-https://www.firststepalliance.org/post/norway-prison-system-lessons

Conclusion:

What are you thinking after reading the all the stories on the previous pages? Shocked? Still feel the same way and feel they don't deserve any pity due to their crimes? I am sure a lot will still feel that way but hopefully it made you think about things a little in a different perspective. It all goes back to what I said in the introduction about us being human. None of these people asked to suffer from their minds. I don't agree with their crimes and I'm not supporting their crimes. I just try to look at the bigger picture and connect the dots to where we can improve the views on mental health.

I've had many prisoners and others tell me how prison officials don't care about helping prisoners out because it racks in money for the prison and state. It's all a money thing like most things are anymore so its good to see some of the positive aspects of things I have included in this book (Story 15 and Cook County Sheriff's Office Mental Health Programs Summary) because it shows there are people out there trying to make a difference.

Before I end this project I am going to

talk about 5 cases that I found interesting and makes you wonder how much mental illness played a part in their crimes and like I said earlier I don't support what they done, but I honestly have to ask myself what if they got the proper help...would it have changed the outcome?

"The United States now has more than 2 million people in prisons or jails--the equivalent of one in every 142 U.S. residents--and another four to five million people on probation or parole. A higher percentage of the population is involved in the criminal justice system in the United States than in any other developed country.

Many inmates have serious mental illnesses. Starting in the late 1950s and 1960s, new psychotropic drugs and the community health movement dramatically reduced the number of people in state mental hospitals. But in the 1980s, many of the mentally ill who had left mental institutions in the previous two decades began entering the criminal justice system.

Today, somewhere between 15 and 20 percent of people in prison are mentally ill, according to U.S. Department of Justice estimates.

"Prisons have really become, in many ways, the de facto mental health hospitals," says former prison psychologist Thomas Fagan, PhD. "But prisons weren't built to deal with mentally ill people; they were built to deal with criminals doing time."

By ETIENNE BENSON
(https://www.apa.org/monitor/julaug03/rehab)

Andre Thomas:

Andre Thomas started hearing voices when he was 9 years old and first tried to kill himself when he was 10. He was filled with religious delusions and hallucinations and it only got worse the older he got.

In March 2004, when he was 21, his mental illness had a breakdown and it resulted in him stabbing his estranged wife and their 4 year old son and her 13 month old daughter (who she had with her boyfriend). He cut the hearts out of the two children. He told police God had instructed him to kill and that he believed his family were demons.

He was sentenced to death after his insanity defense was rejected despite being diagnosed with schizophrenia. The prosecutors argued that he knew what he did was wrong and his mental illness had gotten worse due to drug use. He did drank heavily and used cold medicine leading up to the murders.

He is blind because he gouged out his eyes (the first one being his right eye a few days after the murders), eating one of them to make sure that the government could not hear his thoughts.

I read a day or at least two days before the murders, he had sought help at a local hospital for his delusions and I read he had stabbed himself. He was left alone, and in turn he felt no one was helping him, he left the hospital. I did read the hospital had told police he might have been dangerous but no contact was made with him before the murders. If Andre got help then would those 3 people still be living?

Sources:
-https://nypost.com/2023/02/18/death-row-inmate-andre-thomas-who-cut-out-eyes-ate-one-seeks-clemency
-https://www.texastribune.org/2023/02/15/texas-death-row-andre-thomas/

Richard Chase:

Richard Chase has an interesting case. He earned the nickname *The Vampire of Sacramento* due to him drinking the blood of his victims and eating their internal organs. He did this because of a delusion that he needed to prevent Nazis from turning his blood into powder via poison they had planted beneath his soap dish.

Richard had a handful of girlfriends in high school even though he wasn't able to maintain a steady relationship with them. It was reported he couldn't keep an erection. He consulted a psychiatrist and was told that was root of his problem was due to repressed rage or mental illness. He did not seek anything further after the diagnosis. It was later determined he had an aversion to normal sex. He could only be turned on and orgasm through violent or disturbing acts, such as killing animals and necrophilia.

At one point when he was living alone, he began to capture, kill and disembowel animals and in turn devour them raw. He began to also put the entrails of the animals he had killed into a blender in order to make smoothies. He believed drinking smoothies would prevent his heart from shrinking because he feared if it shrank too much it would disappear and then he would die.

In 1975, he was involuntarily committed to a mental hospital after being taken to a hospital for blood poisoning. He had got blood poisoning after injecting rabbit's blood into his veins.

He would escape from the hospital and went home to his mother. He would be caught again and sent to an institution. There he would share with the staff about his fantasies of killing rabbits. He was once found with blood smeared around his mouth, it was revealed he had caught two birds through the bars on his bedroom window. He snapped their necks and sucked their blood out.

He would have a bunch of treatments done involving psychotropic drugs and would be deemed no longer a threat to society and in 1976, he was released to his parents. The only issue here is his mother decided that her son didn't need to be on the anti-schizophrenic medication and soon weaned him off it.

His parents ended up putting him in an apartment and in no time he was back to his old ways of capturing animals to torture them to death and then drink their blood. A few of the times he even killed and ate his neighbor's pets, and at least once it was reported he had called one of them to tell them what he had done.

At some point during this time is where he would develop a love for guns and decided to buy several handguns. This is when he became fascinated by the crimes of the Hillside Strangler. He believed the Strangler was also a victim of the Nazi/UFO conspiracy that he believed he was a victim of.

His mental health was rapidly getting worse as he began to lose interest in caring for himself. He neglected his personal hygiene by not bathing, grooming and brushing his teeth. He even stopped eating and dropped down to 145 pounds.

There was one incident in 1977, he would rang his mother's doorbell and greeted her by thrusting a dead cat in her face. He then threw the cat to the ground, knelt down, ripped its stomach open with his bare hands, and stuck his hands inside the animal, smearing its blood all over his face while screaming. His mother returned inside the house and never reported the incident to anyone.

There was another strange incident in 1977, the state police discovered his car lodged in a sand drift. There were two rifles, a pile of clothes, a bucket full of blood and a cow's liver. The officer was able to track him down to see he was naked and screaming in the sand, soaked from head to toe in blood. When the officer questioned him, he claimed the blood was his own, and that it had leaked out of him through his flesh. It turned out to be cow's blood.

At the end of the year Richard fired his gun into a kitchen, but luckily noone was hurt in the incident. Two short days later he ended up killing his first victim and the police would match the bullet from the incident that happened two days prior.

In January 1978, he asked his neighbor for a cigarette and then forcible restrained her until she ended up giving him a whole pack.

Two weeks later, he attempted to enter

another house of another woman, but he found her doors locked. He ended up leaving and later told police that he took locked doors as a sign that he was not welcomed, but that unlocked doors were an invitation to come inside. A simple locked door keeping him out...I find that interesting.

He broke into another home where a young married couple lived, he stole some items from them, urinated into a drawer of their infant's clothing, and defecated on their son's bed. The couple came home while he was still there and the husband attacked him...Richard escaped.

He continued to enter into homes until he finally came across a home where the front door was unlocked. The woman was pregnent and home by herself taking out the trash when Richard went into her home. He surprised her and shot her three times. Once in the hand and twice in the head. He took her body into her bedroom and raped it post-mortem while repeatedly stabbing it with a butcher knife. When he finished, he cut the corpse open and removed several of her internal organs, using a bucket to collect the blood and then took it to the bathroom to bathe in it. He then sliced off her nipple and drank her blood. Before he left, he went into the yard, found a pile of dog poop, and returned to stuff it into the corpse's mouth.

Two years after the murder, he purchased two puppies and drank their blood then left the bodies on his neighbor's front yard.

His final murders were just as brutal as the others. He entered the home of a lady who was babysitting her 22 month old nephew, along with her six year old son and a neighbor who had came over to check on her. She was in the bath when Richard entered the home. Richard shot the neighbor in the head at point-blank range. He took his wallet and car keys. The little boy ran to his mother's bedroom, where Richard shot him twice in the head at point-blank range. During this time Richard also shot the nephew in the head.

He entered the bathroom and shot the mother in the head. He took her corpse to the bed where he sodomized it and drank its blood from a series of slices to the back of the neck. Medical examiners reported there was a large amount of semen in her rectum. When he was finished, he stabbed her at least a dozen times in the anus. He sliced open her stomach and drained her blood into a bucket. He consumed all the blood.

He took her neighbor's corpse to the bathroom and split its skull open in the bathtub, and ate some of the brain.

A little girl who the boy had a play-date with knocked on the door, the knock startled Richard so he fled the scene. He took the neighbor's car and the little girl alerted another neighbor of the strange individual. The neighbor went into the house and discovered all the bodies and contacted the police.

Police ended up finding that Richard left perfect hand prints and perfect imprints of his shoes in some of the blood.

Richard had taken the 22 month old nephew's corpse home with him, where he chopped off his penis and used it as a straw to suck the blood out of the body. He cut open the corpse and ate several of the internal organs and made smoothies out of others. He disposed of the corpse at a nearby church. Richard was arrested.

In 1979, Richard was found guilty of six counts of murder. Richard ended up giving a series of interviews while he was locked up to Robert K. Ressler and this is where he talked about his fears of Nazis and UFOs. He asked Robert to give him access to a radar gun, with which he could catch the Nazi UFOs, so the Nazis could stand trial for the murders. He also handed Robert a large amount of macaroni and cheese, which he had been hoarding in his pants pockets. He believed the prison officials were helping the Nazis and attempting to kill him with poisoning his food.

On December 26, 1980, Richard was found dead in his prison cell. It was revealed he had committed suicide from an overdose of prescribed medication.

I find Richard's case so disturbing. It did seem he got some help in the beginning, but then he mother just ignored it and I didn't agree with her weening him off of his medication. Did she feel nothing was wrong with her son? Was she afraid of her family name being ruined with Richard's actions? There is a lot to take in here and I'm still not sure you'd completely understand what Richard was thinking when he did what he did. He probably didn't fully understand it either when it was going on.

Sources:
-https://murderpedia.org/male.C/c/chase-richard.htm

Joshua Rudiger:

Joshua was the son of a homeless drug-addicted prostitute and an unknown father. His psychiatrist said he sank deeper into mental illness despite years of treatment. He reported Josh did not know right from wrong at the time of his crimes. There were records to show him to be psychotic from the age of 4, one diagnosis after another.

He was found in a filthy bathtub at the age of 7 months of his mother's apartment. It seem he had been unattended for two or three days.

He lived in four different foster homes in two years. This was at the time of age 4 when he began banging his head, biting his tongue and forcing himself to vomit. He was diagnosed with mentally retardation and psychosis at the time. It was around this time he began telling doctors he was living a double life in which he saw himself as a ninja warrior.

He continued to live in foster homes until the age of 15, when he tried to kill himself by stabbing himself with a samurai sword. He spent the next eight months in six different psychiatric hospitals. This is where he would sneak out of his room at night and lick the chests of other patients. He had the idea in his head of becoming a vampire and sucking their blood out he told one of his therapists. He left at the age of 18 despite tests showing he was in worse shape than when he went in.

He was sent to a treatment center, but walked away after three months. He was picked up by police not long after carrying a head fish. He told them he was on his way to Japan town in San Francisco because he hoped to use a light to cook ninja sushi.

In 1997, he was arrested for a knife attack on a homeless man. He got lucky because the man died soon afterwards in an unrelated incident. It left no one to testify against him so police had no choice but to release him. This was the time he told the hospital doctors he was a samurai.

In August 1997, he spent six months at a state hospital after a bow and arrow attack on a friend. This is when he was diagnosed with schizophrenic and had bipolar disorder, but despite this, they felt he was fit for trial. The only thing to help him out here is the friend refused to testify against him, which in turn put him on probation and ordered to go to a live-in treatment center.

Soon after, he disappeared and moved to a hotel. Five months after being put on probation he began his attacks on homeless people.

His first victim he slit her throat and drank her blood. She died from lack of blood. The next three weeks another three homeless men unwillingly donated blood to him. They at least survived their neck wounds. He also used their blood to write a Chinese-language symbol for death.

It didn't take long for him to be connected to the attacks. He was arrested and told authorities he had been a samurai in another life who burned down the holiest temple in Japan, killing worshipers, and was punished by God in this life by being forced to drink human blood to maintain his vitality.

At his trial he pleaded not guilty by reason of insanity. You'd think it would work in his case, but the jury rejected it. The prosecutor claimed his mental illness was invented to escape punishment for the attacks. It does seem the jury was looking at the crimes (which were bad) instead of the bigger picture since we know Josh had been diagnosed as mentally incompetent for all of his life.

On May 31, 2020, prison officials found another inmate with multiple stab wounds to the neck in the showers. Guess what? Joshua had been in the showers at the same time. He would be later charged with the murder.

All in all it seem Joshua did get help somewhat early on in his life, but was it enough? It doesn't appear that way because he ended up being known as the "Vampire Slasher" and he claimed himself to be a 2,600 year old vampire.

Check out his interviews on the podcast *Unforbidden Truth* hosted by Andrew Dodge! (available on Youtube and all major podcast platforms).

https://www.youtube.com/@unforbiddentruthpodcast

Sources:

-https://www.latimes.com/california/story/2020-
06-02/self-proclaimed-vampire-suspected-of-
killing-fellow-inmate-in-prison-shower
-https://murderpedia.org/male.R/r/rudiger-
joshua.htm

Andrea Yates

Andrea Yates killed her five children aged 7, 5, 3, 2 and 6 months in June 2001. She drowned all five of them in their bathtub.

She had been suffering for some time with very severe postpartum depression and postpartum psychosis.

The following of the birth of their fourth son, she had become depressed. In June 1999, her husband had found her shaking and chewing on her fingers. The next day she tried to kill herself by overdosing on pills. Once she was released from the hospital after being prescribed antidepressants, she begged her husband to let her die as she held a knife up to her neck. She was hospitalized once again. She was given a mixture of medication and her condition seem to improve rather quickly.

In July 1999, she ended up having a nervous breakdown and two suicide attempts followed along with being in an psychiatric hospital two times during the summer. This is where she was diagnosed with postpartum psychosis.

At one point a psychiatrist urged the

couple not to have anymore children because it would guarantee psychotic depression for Andrea. She ended up pregnant around 7 weeks later after she was discharged. She gave birth to their daughter in November 2000. She seem to be doing okay until the death of her father in March 2001.

She stopped taking her medication, mutilated herself, and read the Bible religiously. During this time she stopped feeding their youngest child. She became so bad off that she required to be hospitalized again.

She was treated and released to only go back into a bad state of mind where she would fill the bathtub up in the middle of the day. She later confessed to police that she had planned to drown her children then, but had decided against it. She was hospitalized the next day and it was determined she was probably suicidal and the tub was actually for her to drown herself.

Andrea ended up being left alone after her husband left for work. The doctor has instructed for her to never be left alone. Andrea's mother was scheduled to arrive an hour after her husband left for work to take care of Andrea, but in that hour Andrea was able to drown all their children. She called the police afterwards and then her husband saying only "it's time" over and over.

The Call:

911 Dispatcher "What's your name?"
Andrea Yates: "Andrea Yates."
911 Dispatcher "What's the problem?"
Andrea Yates: "Um, I just need him to come."
911 Dispatcher "Is your husband there?"
Andrea Yates: "No."
911 Dispatcher "Well, what's the problem?"
Andrea Yates: "I need him to come."
911 Dispatcher "I need to know why we're coming, ma'am. Is he there standing next to you?"
Andrea Yates: "No."
911 Dispatcher "She?"
Andrea Yates: "Pardon me?"
911 Dispatcher "Are you having a disturbance? Are you ill or what?"
Andrea Yates: "Um, yes, I'm ill."
911 Dispatcher "Do you need an ambulance?"

Andrea Yates: "No, I need a police officer.
Yeah, send an ambulance."
911 Dispatcher "What's the problem?"
Andrea Yates: "Um?"
911 Dispatcher "Hello?"
Andrea Yates: "I just need a police officer."

While in prison, she had thought about killing her children for 2 years because she thought she was not a good mother and claimed her kids were developing improperly.

She had stated it was the 7th deadly sin. She said they stumbled because she was evil. She felt they couldn't be saved because of how she was raising them. She felt they were doomed to perish in the fires of hell. She also added Satan influenced her children and made them more disobedient.

She was sentenced to 40 years in prison with a possibility of parole afterwards in 2002. Her sentence was overturned in 2006 and she was found not guilty by reason of insanity.

Since January 2007, she has been at a hospital (mentally facility) in Texas. She can undergo a review every year to see if she is competent to leave the facility. She opts each year to waive her right to be reviewed. It has been confirmed she has never undergone a review. She instead chose to continue the treatment she is receiving.

Sources:
-https://murderpedia.org/female.Y/y/yates-andrea.htm
-https://people.com/crime/andrea-yates-who-drowned-kids-in-bathtub-in-2001-annually-declines-release-from-mental-hospital/

Robert "Bobby" Joe Long:

Bobby nearly drowned in 1957 at 4 years old. He fell off a swing in 1958 and crashed his bicycle into a parked vehicle in 1959. He injuried his head after he fell from a pony he was riding, resulting in dizziness and nausea for several weeks. His last incident resulting in major head trauma was after he had enlisted in the army. He crashed his motorcycle 6 months in, shattering his helmet with the impact of his skull on the road.

In 1980, he received a diagnosis of "Traumatic Brian Disease" from the VA (Veterans Administration) as a result of the wreck he had during his military service. He was discharged, but sadly only received little to no treatment from the military or the VA for his brain damage.

He suffered headaches and unpredictable violent rages and his sexual urges increased. While still in a cast, he masturbated five times a day to relieve himself. He continued even at home despite having his wife have sex with him multiple times a day.

His daughter claimed after the wreck

about his personality had changed. His ex-wife was stating how he had changed after the accident.

"He would tell me what to do, what to eat, how to act...he got to the point where he would start smacking me in the face or smacking me in the back of the head. Two or three times, he choked me so bad I lost consciousness."

-His ex-wife

"I was so…"insane" with anger!!! She pushed me to it. I begged her to…"shut up! Stop! Let it Drop!" and when she wouldn't, I lost it (I was 25-26?)…I almost killed the girl I loved, the mother of our 2 babies, asleep in the next room. She never saw, or felt the same way about me, after that. It's one of the things I'm sorriest about ————in a long list of things!!! ————In my life. I shoulda treated her… better..every day I was lucky enough to have her in my life."

The struggle of feeding the sexual hunger he gained, he began to look for other prey. He eventually became known as the "Classified Ad Rapist". In 1981, he answered ads for small appliances, and if he found a woman or young girl alone at home he would rape them. He is suspected of at least 50 rapes and I have seen the number grow as high as 100.

In 1984, he began killing for a 8 month time period. He was charged with 9 counts of first-degree murder. He was suspected of a 10th victim, but was never charged against him. Some he strangled, others he cut their throats or bludgeoned them to death. The bodies were placed in unique positions and left out in various locations. Five of the victims were identified as prostitutes, two as exotic dancers, one was a factory worker, one was a student, and one was of unknown occupation.

The reason he was caught was because he kidnapped a 17 year old girl off the street. He kept her for 26 hours where he raped her repeatedly, but decided to let her go and this is where he was able to remember details of his car among other things to get him finally arrested.

I don't condone his crimes and what he did. He deserved what he got, but I do want to point out that during his trial medical experts testified that his head injuries (especially motorcycle wreck) had damaged the areas of the brain responsible for judgment and behavior control.

"Starting back in March, the outgoing gov. and his EVIL little bitch of an attorney general put me in the cross-hairs, and want to GET me before they have to leave office in Jan. (Due to term limits.) They up a "clemency interview" in Sept., which on the advice of counsel—I refused to participate in. As soon as they deny me a full "Clemency Hearing" they can sign a death warrant on me. The whole clemency things a joke. Fla. Hasn't granted a death row prisoner clemency in 40 years. And really, I have no interest in clemency, or a life sentence. It's gonna be interesting to see how it all works out. Lottsa related LEGAL-shit going on, as well. But I won't bore you to sleep, with

all that. Not sure how much longer I'll be around. Just thought you oughtta know. And really, it doesn't matter much, anymore, either way."

-Email from Bobby
(This was the last time I heard from him in October 2018. He got the lethal injection in May 2019).

Sources:
-https://www.grunge.com/432377/what-serial-killer-bobby-joe-longs-childhood-was-really-like/
-https://murderpedia.org/male.L/l/long-bobby-joe.htm
-https://deathpenaltyinfo.org/news/florida-executes-mentally-ill-vietnam-veteran-diagnosed-with-traumatic-brain-disease
-https://www.tyla.com/entertaining/tv-and-film-bobby-joe-long-daughter-sarah-crosby-brain-injury-personality-change-20210609

Acknowledgments:

I want to thank everyone who is in this book without you all this wouldn't have been accomplished. I also want to thank my lady Olivia because she listened to me daily with my thoughts/ideas and her patience seeing me work on this for the time it took to put it all together. Thank you all!

Other Books by Bruce LeMaster:
(All books available on Amazon)

-Phillip Jablonski: The Death Row Teddy Bear (2020)
-A Bible On Death Row (2021)
-The Terrifying Toolbox Murders (2021)
-Odds and Ends of Ted Bundy (2021)
-West Virginia Missing (2022)

Future Projects:
-The Wolf and The Killer: Volume 1 (Coming late 2023 or early 2024)
-The Wolf and The Killer: Volume 2 (Coming 2024)

Contact:

Check out the page Killer's Crawlspace on Facebook, Twitter, Instagram, Tiktok and Youtube to keep up with updates!

-killerscrawlspace.wordpress.com (Blog)
-killerscrawlspace.podbean.com (Podcast/also available most places you get your podcasts at)
-www.youtube.com/@killerscrawlspace1924

Please leave a review on Amazon or Goodreads!

9 798359 122467